FOLK HEROES

Annie Oakley

JILL FORAN

AV² provides enriched content that supplements and complements this book. Weigl's AV² books strive to create inspired learning and engage young minds in a total learning experience.

Your AV² Media Enhanced books come alive with...

Audio
Listen to sections of the book read aloud.

Key Words
Study vocabulary, and complete a matching word activity.

Video
Watch informative video clips.

Quizzes
Test your knowledge.

Go to **www.av2books.com**, and enter this book's unique code.

BOOK CODE

AVX43472

Embedded Weblinks
Gain additional information for research.

Slide Show
View images and captions, and prepare a presentation.

AV² by Weigl brings you media enhanced books that support active learning.

Try This!
Complete activities and hands-on experiments.

... and much, much more!

Published by AV² by Weigl
350 5th Avenue, 59th Floor
New York, NY 10118
Website: www.av2books.com

Library of Congress Cataloging-in-Publication Data
Names: Foran, Jill, author.
Title: Annie Oakley / Jill Foran.
Description: New York : AV2 by Weigl, [2019] | Series: Folk Heroes | Includes
  webography. | Includes index.
Identifiers: LCCN 2018051727 (print) | LCCN 2018054162 (ebook) | ISBN
  9781489695703 (Multi User ebook) | ISBN 9781489695710 (Single User ebook)
  | ISBN 9781489695680 (hardcover : alk. paper) | ISBN 9781489695697(softcover : alk. paper)
Subjects: LCSH: Oakley, Annie, 1860-1926--Juvenile literature. | Shooters of
  firearms--United States--Biography--Juvenile literature. |
  Entertainers--United States--Biography--Juvenile literature.
Classification: LCC GV1157.03 (ebook) | LCC GV1157.03 F67 2019 (print) | DDC
  799.3/1092--dc23
LC record available at https://lccn.loc.gov/2018051727

Printed in Guangzhou, China
1 2 3 4 5 6 7 8 9 0 23 22 21 20 19

012019
130118

Project Coordinator: Heather Kissock
Art Director: Terry Paulhus

Photo Credits
Every reasonable effort has been made to trace ownership and to obtain permission to reprint copyright material. The publishers would be pleased to have any errors or omissions brought to their attention so that they may be corrected in subsequent printings. Weigl acknowledges Alamy, Getty Images, and Bridgeman Images as its primary image suppliers for this title.

Annie Oakley

CONTENTS

On Target

Annie Oakley was a champion **markswoman**. She showed audiences from around the world that she could shoot almost anything. Annie was a natural performer. She was also a kind and generous person. When she finished performing, she had her gold medals melted. She sold the gold and gave the money to poor people.

Annie lived during a time when it was believed that women should not shoot guns for sport. Still, she became one of the most respected and talented **sharpshooters** in history.

"Aim at a high mark and you will hit it."
– Annie Oakley

Annie's real name was Phoebe Ann Mosey. "Annie Oakley" was the name she used when she performed in front of audiences.

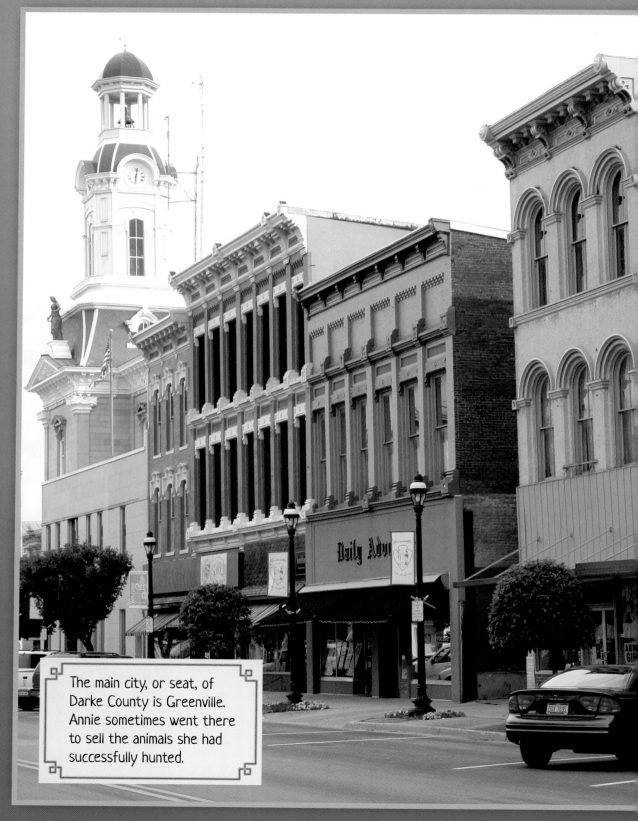

The main city, or seat, of Darke County is Greenville. Annie sometimes went there to sell the animals she had successfully hunted.

Folk Heroes

Growing Up

Annie Oakley was born in Darke County, Ohio, on August 13, 1860. Her parents were hard-working farmers. Annie was only 5 years old when her father died of **pneumonia**. Life became difficult for the family after his death. Annie's mother had very little money because there were seven children to feed. Annie taught herself how to use her father's gun so that she could hunt animals for food. She hit a squirrel the first time she went hunting.

Annie was sent to live on a farm when she was 8 years old. This farm housed and supported poor people and children who did not have parents to care for them. Then, Annie worked as a servant for a local family to make money to help her mother. Annie did not return to live with her own family for several years.

"For me, sitting still is harder than any kind of work."
– Annie Oakley

Shooting Skills

By the time she was 15 years old, Annie was making a great deal of money for her family. She earned this money by hunting and selling **game**. Annie was a great hunter even as a young girl. People began to notice her shooting skills. She was soon invited to take part in a shooting contest. She competed against a famous marksman named Frank Butler. Everyone was surprised when Annie won the contest. However, Annie did not just win the shooting competition. She also won Frank Butler's heart. Frank and Annie fell in love. They were married on August 23, 1876.

Annie went on to win many more contests. She earned hundreds of awards and medals for her shooting skills.

Annie won the shooting contest by a score of one. She shot 25 clay disks. Frank shot 24.

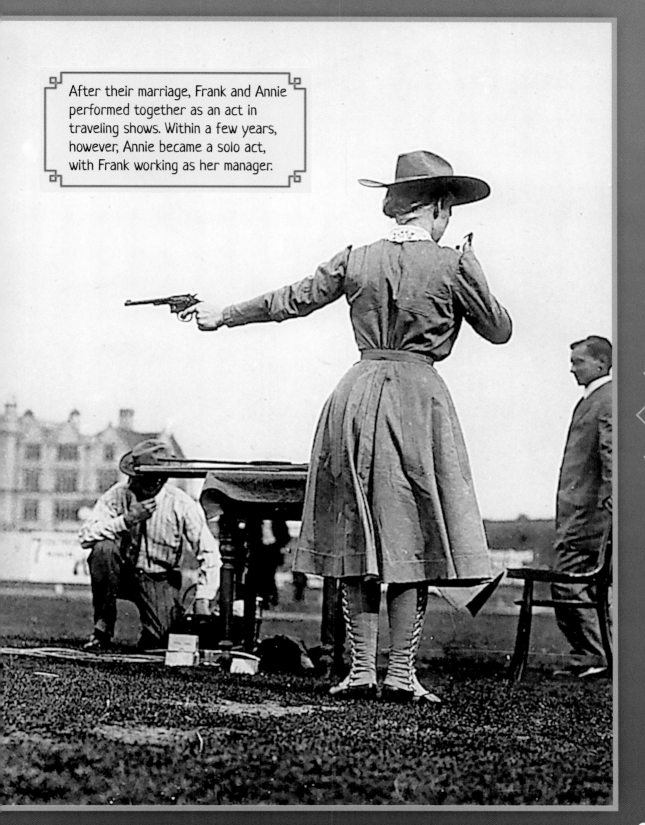

After their marriage, Frank and Annie performed together as an act in traveling shows. Within a few years, however, Annie became a solo act, with Frank working as her manager.

Playing cards were a key part of Annie's act. In some cases, she shot a card in half. In others, she shot a hole through the center of a card.

A Shooting Superstar

Annie Oakley soon became one of the best markswomen in the world. She was skilled at using shotguns, **rifles**, and pistols. Annie was an expert shooter. People loved to tell stories about unbelievable targets that Annie had hit. Many stories were exaggerated, but some were true.

Audiences watched Annie shoot a dime that had been tossed into the air 90 feet (27 meters) away. Annie could shoot out a candle flame. She could also shoot an apple off her dog's head. Annie could even hit her targets while standing on the back of a running horse.

"While shooting, I...look straight at the object to be fired at, and the moment the butt of the gun touches my shoulder I fire."

– Annie Oakley

The Look of a Legend

Annie was quite small. She stood only 5 feet (1.5 m) tall and weighed about 100 pounds (45 kilograms). Annie's small size made her look very elegant. Annie seemed graceful even when she was handling a 10-pound shotgun. Annie wore **modest** costumes for her performances. She designed and sewed her costumes herself. Her hard work was appreciated. Audiences loved Annie's sporty, ladylike appearance.

Think About It

A person's clothing can say a great deal about them. What do Annie's clothes say about her? Why did Annie pull her hair back? Why was her skirt knee-length? What would you wear if you lived in the 1800s? Think about why each clothing item would be important to a performer.

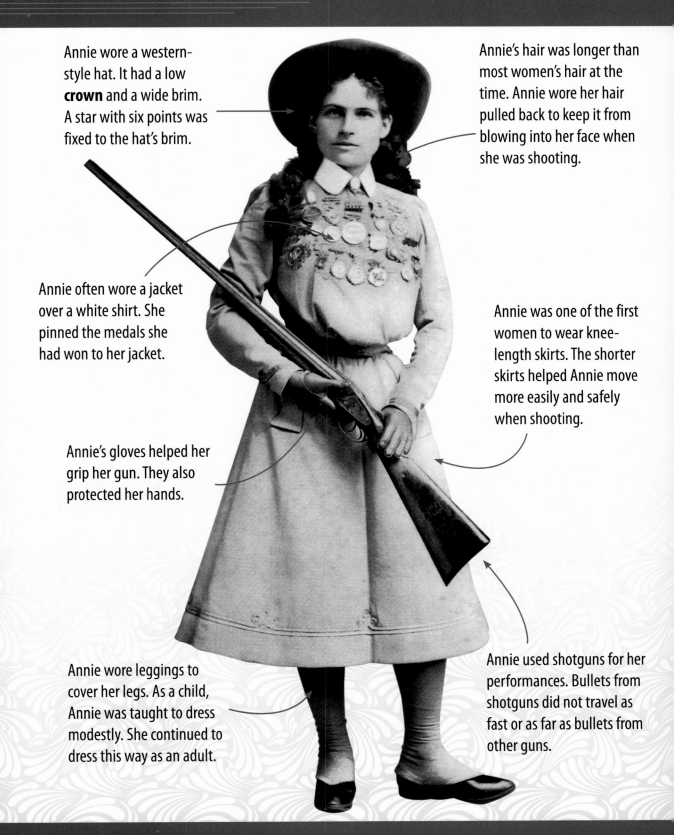

Annie wore a western-style hat. It had a low **crown** and a wide brim. A star with six points was fixed to the hat's brim.

Annie's hair was longer than most women's hair at the time. Annie wore her hair pulled back to keep it from blowing into her face when she was shooting.

Annie often wore a jacket over a white shirt. She pinned the medals she had won to her jacket.

Annie was one of the first women to wear knee-length skirts. The shorter skirts helped Annie move more easily and safely when shooting.

Annie's gloves helped her grip her gun. They also protected her hands.

Annie wore leggings to cover her legs. As a child, Annie was taught to dress modestly. She continued to dress this way as an adult.

Annie used shotguns for her performances. Bullets from shotguns did not travel as fast or as far as bullets from other guns.

The Wild West

Annie gave many thrilling performances during her career. In 1885, she joined a show called Buffalo Bill's Wild West. Buffalo Bill's real name was William Cody. He was a famous hunter and showman. His show toured in the United States, Canada, and Europe. Buffalo Bill's Wild West featured talented horseback riders, skilled **ropers**, and sharpshooters. The show also featured a **legendary Sioux** chief named Sitting Bull.

Buffalo Bill and Sitting Bull gave Annie special nicknames because she was so small. Buffalo Bill called her "Little Missie." Sitting Bull called her "Little Sure Shot."

In 1887, Buffalo Bill's Wild West performed for Great Britain's Queen Victoria. When the queen met Annie, she called her "a very clever girl."

The Western Girl

Annie Oakley became one of the most popular Western performers in the world. Many books and plays were written about her. In 1902 and 1903, Annie starred in a play called *The Western Girl*. It was written especially for her.

Audiences continued to be interested in Annie even after her death in 1926. A **musical** called *Annie Get Your Gun* was written in the 1940s. It celebrated her life and skills. A television show called *Annie Oakley* was popular in the 1950s.

Today, Annie Oakley is honored in the National Cowgirl Museum and Hall of Fame in Fort Worth, Texas. It is the only museum in the world to honor cowgirls, ranch women, writers, artists, teachers, and entertainers of the West.

The Garst Museum in Greenville, Ohio, has the world's largest collection of Annie Oakley artifacts.

Annie Get Your Gun was made into a movie in 1950. It won an Academy Award for its music.

Timeline of Annie Oakley

1860
Annie Oakley is born in Darke County, Ohio. Her real name is Phoebe Ann Mosey.

1876
Annie marries Frank Butler.

1866
Annie's father dies.

1901
Annie hurts her back in a train accident. She must have five operations.

1885
Annie joins Buffalo Bill's Wild West show.

1887
Queen Victoria of Great Britain celebrates her fiftieth year as queen. The Wild West show travels to Britain. Annie performs for the British royal.

Annie Oakley had humble beginnings, but her shooting skills took her around the world. Everywhere she went, people flocked to see her shoot seemingly impossible targets. Over time, her legend grew, helping to make her the folk hero she is today.

1917
The United States enters World War I. Annie writes to the government offering to train the female soldiers. The government never replies to her letter.

1917 to 1918
Annie and Frank help the government during the war. They give shooting lessons to soldiers.

1922
Annie and Frank are hurt in a car accident. Annie breaks her hip and her ankle. She must wear a leg brace for the rest of her life.

1926
Annie Oakley dies of a blood disease on November 3. Frank Butler dies 18 days later.

1

In which state was Annie Oakley born?

a) Colorado
b) Wyoming
c) Ohio
d) Nebraska

2

Which famous show did Annie tour with for almost 17 years?

a) The Western Girl
b) Buffalo Bill's Wild West
c) Annie Get Your Gun
d) Annie Oakley

What Have You Learned?

Test your knowledge of Annie Oakley by answering the following questions.

3

Which nickname did Sitting Bull give to Annie?

a) "Little Missie"
b) "America's Sweetheart"
c) "Phoebe Ann"
d) "Little Sure Shot"

4

True or False?
Annie married Buffalo Bill after she beat him in a shooting competition.

5

True or False?
Annie was one of the first women to wear knee-length skirts.

6

True or False?
Annie was almost 6 feet (1.8 m) tall.

7

True or False?
Annie wore a six-pointed star on her hat.

8

True or False?
Annie wore gloves because she had small fingers.

10

True or False?
Annie took shooting lessons.

9

True or False?
Most women in the 1800s shot guns for sport.

Compare and Contrast

Annie Oakley was not like the other women of her time. How was Annie's life different from the lives of the other women living during the 1800s? Use the library or the internet to find out how Annie was different from the other women of her time. Research the ways in which Annie was similar to the other women of her time. Create a chart or a poster that shows what you have learned.

Key Words

crown: the highest part, the top

game: wild animals that are hunted for sport, money, or food

legendary: featured in stories that cannot be proven to be true

markswoman: woman skilled in shooting at targets

modest: plain and simple

musical: a play that contains songs and dances

pneumonia: an illness of the lungs

rifles: guns that have a long barrel and are fired from the shoulder

ropers: people who catch animals or objects using ropes

sharpshooters: people who are good at shooting guns

Sioux: a Native American group

Index

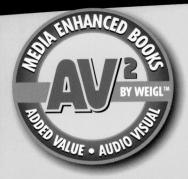

Log on to www.av2books.com

AV² by Weigl brings you media enhanced books that support active learning. Go to www.av2books.com, and enter the special code found on page 2 of this book. You will gain access to enriched and enhanced content that supplements and complements this book. Content includes video, audio, weblinks, quizzes, a slideshow, and activities.

AV² Online Navigation

Audio
Listen to sections of the book read aloud.

Book Pages
AV² pages directly correspond to pages in the book.

Video
Watch informative video clips.

Key Words
Study vocabulary, and complete a matching word activity.

Embedded Weblinks
Gain additional information for research.

Quizzes
Test your knowledge.

Slideshow
View images and captions, and prepare a presentation.

Try This!
Complete activities and hands-on experiments.

AV² was built to bridge the gap between print and digital. We encourage you to tell us what you like and what you want to see in the future.

Sign up to be an AV² Ambassador at www.av2books.com/ambassador.